Contents

continued on next page

CELEBRATION PRESS
Pearson Learning Group

The following people have contributed to the development of this product:

Art and Design: John Maddalone, Liz Nemeth, Evelyn O'Shea

Editorial: Linette Mathewson

Inventory: Yvette Higgins

Marketing: Ken Clinton

Production/Manufacturing: Michele Uhl

Publishing Operations: Richetta Lobban

COVER ART: John Maddalone

ISBN 0-7652-7567-8

Printed in the United States of America
7 8 9 10   09 08

Celebration Press

Pearson Learning Group

1-800-321-3106
www.pearsonlearning.com

counted	laughed	reached	started
shaped	leaned	shouted	screamed
closed	stared	pleased	raised
stepped	shipped	grabbed	wrapped
supplied	emptied	married	buried
swatted	matted	shaded	skated
studied	replied	hurried	shopped

Review Inflected Ending -ed

Change -y to i	Double	Drop e	No Change
worried	starred	changed	learned

Read the base words in the box. Make new words by adding the ending -ed to each base word. (Drop e, double the final letter, and change -y to i as necessary.) Write each new word on a line in the correct column.

supply	lean	shape	worry	reach	please	empty	shout	hurry	mat	reply
step	learn	star	bury	raise	grab	count	scream	swat	study	change
close	marry	wrap	start	laugh	ship	stare	skate	shop	shade	

No Change

Drop e

Double

Change -y to i

reorder	distrust	reinstall	unread
misplace	disorder	reconsider	mislead
disapprove	misconduct	unheated	mistrust
reassure	unplanned	discomfort	unattached
reaction	unglued	misstep	disagree

mis-					
misfortune					

dis-					
discontinue					

un-					
unopened					

re-					
repackage					

Sort 2: Review Prefixes re-, un-, dis-, mis-

9

Complete each sentence by adding the prefix re-, un-, dis-, or mis- to the base word in parentheses. Write the word on the line.

1. Alvaro had to _____ the software after his computer crashed. (install)

2. When your room is messy, it is easy to _____ something. (place)

3. Telling Beth that the roller coaster is safe will _____ her. (assure)

4. The sole of his shoe fell off after it came _____. (glued)

5. A tricky person may _____ you. (lead)

6. Our mother will _____ of us staying out so late. (approve)

7. Sam made a _____ on the rocky ground. (step)

8. The engine was _____ and could not pull the train. (attached)

9. I had to _____ paper for the office when we ran out. (order)

10. We were very cold because the room was _____. (heated)

11. The sports player was benched for _____. (conduct)

12. After Lance's injury, he couldn't hide the _____ from his face. (comfort)

13. It was unlike our family to partake in _____ trips. (planned)

14. When there is _____, our teacher separates the noisy students. (order)

15. Kylie's music teacher encouraged her to _____ the singing competition. (consider)

Review Prefixes uni-, mono-, bi-, tri-

unify	bimonthly	triathlon	unit
monotony	unite	uniform	university
bicycle	binoculars	monorail	tricolor
trimonthly	monologue	bifocal	monotone
trilogy	monogram	unique	biennial
biannual	monopoly	tricycle	triceratops

Sort 3: Review Prefixes uni-, mono-, bi-, tri-

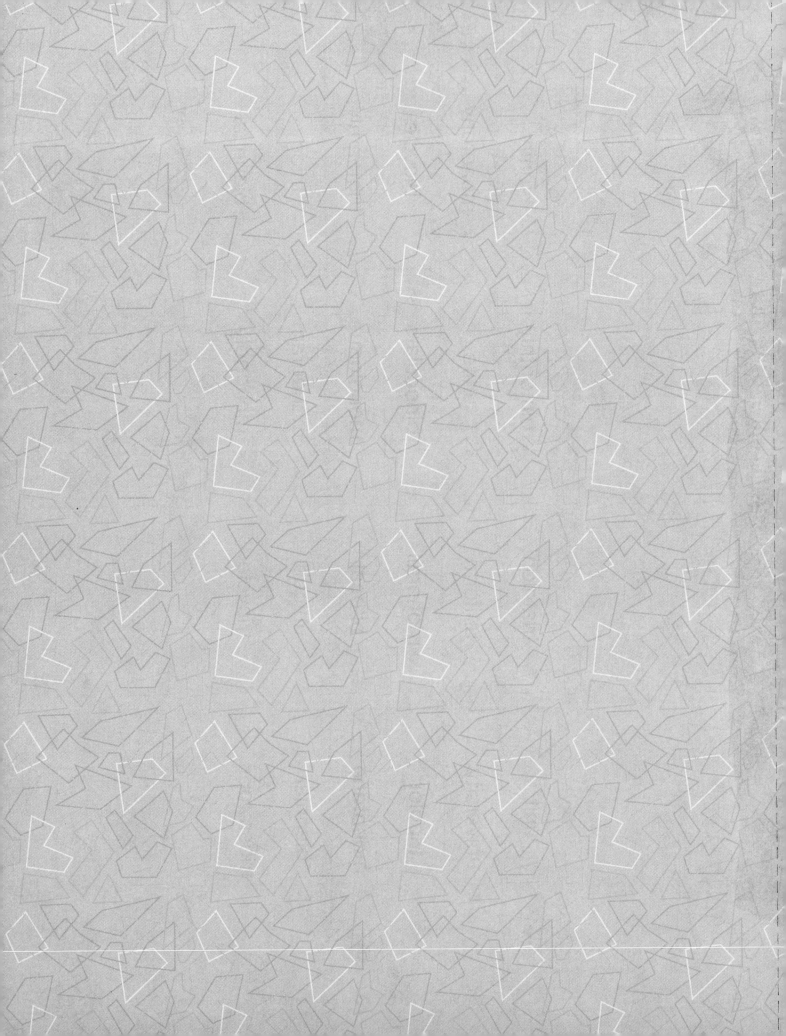

Review Prefixes uni-, mono-, bi-, tri-

tri- triangle							

bi- bilingual							

mono- monolingual							

uni- unison							

Sort 3: Review Prefixes uni-, mono-, bi-, tri-

(13)

1. Write the definition of each prefix.
2. Write a word containing that prefix.
3. Draw a picture to illustrate the word.

uni-: _____

Word: _____

mono-: _____

Word: _____

bi-: _____

Word: _____

tri-: _____

Word: _____

stranger	cleaner	fancier
harshest	hungriest	quietest
trickiest	shiniest	louder
harsher	hungrier	fanciest
trickier	shinier	busiest
loudest	earliest	dullest

cleanest
quieter
earlier
strangest
busier
duller

Review Comparative Suffixes -er, -est, -ier, -iest

-er	-est	-ier	-iest
kinder	kindest	emptier	emptiest

Read each base word. Then write a sentence for each that uses in context either the -er or the -est form of the word. (Change -y to i and drop e as necessary.)

1. tricky _____

2. hungry _____

3. strange _____

4. quiet _____

5. shiny _____

6. clean _____

7. busy _____

8. early _____

9. harsh _____

10. fancy _____

Choose one of the above words and write a sentence using both the -er and -est form of the same word.

_____
_____

fondness	graceful	restless
beautiful	skillfulness	politeness
truthful	priceless	friendliness
fanciful	flawless	emptiness
careful	tireless	respectful
speechless	darkness	grateful
kindness	worthless	breathless
flawlessness	delightful	thoughtlessness

Review Suffixes -ness, -ful, -less

-ness	-ful	-less	Combination of Suffixes
neatness	useful	useless	usefulness

1. Read each sentence. Choose one word from the box that best completes the sentence. (Note: Not all words have to be used and each word can be used only once.)

2. Add the suffix -ness, -ful, -less, or a combination of these suffixes to the word and write it on the line. (Change -y to i as necessary.)

thought	worth	breath	grace	flaw	fancy	kind	skill
delight	friend	respect	dark	fond	speech	polite	care
beauty	price	rest	tire	truth	grateful	empty	neat

1. The stitching on the designer gown was _____.

2. You have to be _____ when walking on ice.

3. Michael was too _____ to sleep.

4. The fake money was completely _____.

5. The flowers in the meadow were very _____.

6. We were _____ when the principal visited our class.

7. Without a flashlight it is hard to walk in _____.

8. The dog showed its _____ by wagging its tail.

9. She is so _____ that she never trips or falls.

10. I was impressed by his _____ when he remembered my birthday.

11. I became _____ while running to the bus.

12. Listening to the holiday concert was _____.

confess	election	correct
possession	collect	depression
discuss	correction	impress
confession	instruct	process
selection	discussion	select
collection	instruction	procession
protect	inspect	protection
possess	inspection	elect
depress	impression	

Adding -ion (With No Spelling Change)

-ss + -ion	Base -ss	-ct + -ion	Base -ct
expression	express	subtraction	subtract

Read each sentence. Choose one word from the pair in parentheses that best completes the sentence and write it on the line. Place an n above the nouns and a v above the verbs.

1. We scheduled an _____ for our car. (inspect/inspection)

2. That rare baseball card is my _____. (possess/possession)

3. The fifth graders will vote to _____ a new class president. (elect/election)

4. I have 150 marbles in my _____. (collect/collection)

5. A mother bear will always try to _____ her cubs. (protect/protection)

6. At the end of the day, the bank tellers _____ the checks. (process/procession)

7. We had a _____ about ways to help people in our community. (discuss/discussion)

8. With so many delicious foods, it's hard to _____ my favorite! (select/selection)

9. The _____ on his face was one of pure joy. (express/expression)

10. This summer my father will _____ the swim team at our town pool. (instruct/instruction)

11. The seashell left a perfect _____ in the sand. (impress/impression)

12. Our teacher asked the class to _____ who left the gift on her desk. (confess/confession)

Sort 6: Adding -ion (With No Spelling Change)

Adding -ion and -ian (With No Spelling Change)

electric	musician	interrupt	digestion
suggestion	optician	invention	exhaust
clinician	adoption	digest	clinic
suggest	optic	invent	music
interruption	adopt	electrician	exhaustion

Adding -ion and -ian (With No Spelling Change)

-ic + -ian	Base -ic	-t + -ion	Base -t
magician	magic	prevention	prevent

1. Read each sentence.
2. Complete each sentence by adding the ending -ion or -ian to the word in parentheses and write the word on the line. Before adding the ending, think about if the word refers to a person who does something.

1. When the power went out we had to call an _____. (electric)

2. She practiced her violin every day to become a better _____. (music)

3. The _____ studied only certain diseases. (clinic)

4. Pardon the _____, but I need an answer now. (interrupt)

5. The _____ entertained the children at the party. (magic)

6. The scientist's new _____ was a robot that can clean floors. (invent)

7. Sitting still can help the _____ of whatever you just ate. (digest)

8. My _____ checks my eyesight twice a year. (optic)

9. We liked her _____ so much that we followed it immediately. (suggest)

10. We had to put my cat's kittens up for _____. (adopt)

11. After the race, all the runners showed their _____. (exhaust)

12. As part of fire _____ week, we practiced exiting the school quickly. (prevent)

Sort 8

reproduce	creation	calculate
introduction	hibernation	fascinate
coordination	reduction	concentration
generation	decorate	reproduction
imitation	coordinate	reduce
imitate	concentrate	create
calculation	generate	hibernate
decoration	fascination	introduce

Drop e + -tion	Base -ce	Drop e + -ion	Base -te
production	produce	location	locate

Make new words by adding -ion to the following base words. (Drop e and make spelling changes as necessary.) Then write a definition of the new word.

1. create _____ Definition: _____

2. introduce _____ Definition: _____

3. coordinate _____ Definition: _____

4. reduce _____ Definition: _____

5. fascinate _____ Definition: _____

6. decorate _____ Definition: _____

7. imitate _____ Definition: _____

8. generate _____ Definition: _____

9. reproduce _____ Definition: _____

10. hibernate _____ Definition: _____

11. concentrate _____ Definition: _____

12. calculate _____ Definition: _____

Sort 8: Adding -ion (With Drop e and Spelling Change)

persuade	decision	emit
omission	division	permission
intrude	invade	transmission
collide	invasion	omit
submission	divide	conclusion
erode	intrusion	transmit
erosion	persuasion	emission
decide	collision	submit
permit	conclude	

Adding -ion (With Predictable Changes in Consonants)

-it > -ission	Base -it	-de > -sion	Base -de
admission	admit	explosion	explode

1. Read each sentence. Choose a base word from the box that best completes the sentence. (Note: Not all words have to be used and each word can be used only once.)

2. Add -ion to the word. (Drop -de and -t and add -sion and -ssion as necessary.) Write the word on the line.

persuade	transmit	emit	permit	admit
conclude	erode	collide	invade	explode
divide	omit	submit	decide	intrude

1. The _____ damaged both cars.

2. By using _____, Randy convinced his mother to let him go out.

3. _____ is wearing away the banks of the river.

4. We decided upon equal _____ of cookies between students.

5. Emma asked the teacher for _____ to leave class.

6. _____ of information via the internet is becoming more common.

7. He was angry at the _____ of his name from the program.

8. The _____ of light from streetlights can make it hard to see stars.

9. The army fought but could not stop their enemy's _____.

10. I read the _____ to see how the book would end.

11. My parents paid for my _____ to the movies.

12. Jamal worked hard on his poetry _____ for the contest.

Adding the Suffix -ation (With Drop e and No Spelling Change)

adapt	relaxation	quotation	tax
civilization	civilize	starvation	quote
adaptation	plantation	exploration	tempt
consider	explore	starve	temptation
consideration	information	imagination	imagine
memorization	organize	plant	inform
taxation	relax	organization	memorize

Sort 10: Adding Suffix -ation (With Drop e and No Spelling Change)   (39)

Drop e + -ation	Base Word	-ation	Base Word
sensation	sense	indentation	indent

1. Read each base word.
2. Add the suffix -ation and write the word on the line. (Drop e as necessary.)
3. Then write a sentence that uses the new word in context.

1. civilize _____
2. explore _____
3. starve _____
4. relax _____
5. quote _____
6. tempt _____
7. consider _____
8. memorize _____
9. sense _____
10. adapt _____
11. imagine _____
12. organize _____

Sort 10: Adding Suffix -ation (With Drop e and No Spelling Change)

moist	limb	bombard	haste
muscle	crumb	resignation	limber
columnist	column	soften	designate
hasten	soft	crumble	resign
bomb	moisten	design	muscular

Silent Consonant	Sounded Consonant
sign	signature

1. Read the words in the box.
2. Write each word in the column that shows whether it has a silent or sounded consonant.
3. Underline the consonants that alternate between silent and sounded.

bomb	moist	crumb	design	muscle
resignation	designate	muscular	limb	moisten
crumble	limber	hasten	haste	soften
bombard	columnist	soft	column	resign

Silent Consonant	Sounded Consonant

Vowel Alternation: Long to Short

breath	revise	athlete	mine
natural	criminal	revision	breathe
athletic	mineral	crime	nation
nature	national	ignite	grateful
ignition	gratitude	precision	precise

Long Vowel	Short Vowel
type	typical

1. Read each sentence.
2. Choose one word from the pair in parentheses that best completes the sentence and write it on the line.
3. Place a long vowel symbol (ˉ) over the long vowels. Place a short vowel symbol (˘) over the short vowels.

1. Esteban had few errors to _____ on his written report. (revise/revision)

2. High in the mountains it is harder to _____. (breath/breathe)

3. Taylor is so _____ that she can run a mile in 6 minutes. (athlete/athletic)

4. Andy showed his _____ for the present by writing a thank-you note. (grateful/gratitude)

5. I left _____ directions so Sue would know where to find us. (precise/precision)

6. They dig up gold and silver in this _____. (mine/mineral)

7. Turning the key in the _____ will start the car. (ignite/ignition)

8. Breaking into someone's house is a _____. (crime/criminal)

9. The company delivers its product to people all across the _____. (nation/national)

10. The _____ home for a bear is the woods. (nature/natural)

Vowel Alternation: Long to Short or /ə/

relative	reptilian	rite
mineral	definition	define
reside	competition	flammable
mine	reptile	confidence
residence	ritual	relate
		majority

compete
natural
flame
confide
nature
major

Vowel Alternation: Long to Short or /ə/

Base Word Long Vowel	Derived Word Short Vowel		Base Word Long Vowel	Derived Word /ə/	
cave	cavity		compose	composition	

Sort 13: Vowel Alternation: Long to Short or /ə/ (53)

1. Read each sentence.
2. Choose one word from the box that best completes the sentence and write it on the line. (Note: Not all words have to be used and each word can be used only once.)
3. Place a short vowel symbol (˘) over the short vowels. Circle the vowels with the schwa sound.

flammable	compose	reptile	definition	compete	composition	relate
mine	rite	relative	reptilian	confidence	nature	cave
ritual	majority	competition	major	reside	confide	
residence	mineral	natural	flame	cavity	define	

1. Can you _____ this word for me?

2. The _____ of marriage is an important ceremony.

3. We were determined to win the _____.

4. The coach showed her _____ in Gabrielle by asking her to lead the warm-up.

5. The _____ of the class attended the baseball playoffs.

6. Do you _____ in this city?

7. The pianist also likes to _____ his own music.

8. We explored the underground _____.

9. Javier admired the color of the _____.

10. The couple prefers a _____ setting for their wedding.

11. A snake is a kind of _____.

12. Gasoline is a _____ substance.

Sort
14

familiar	inspire	familiarity
combine	translate	perspire
preparation	combination	mobile
oppose	mobility	opposition
translation	perspiration	metallic
inspiration	prepare	metal

Base Word	Derived Word
similar	similarity

1. Complete each sentence by adding a new ending to the word in parentheses.
2. Write the derived word on the line.
3. Underline the stressed syllable in each derived word.

1. We showed our _____ to the plan by voting "no." (oppose)

2. Thanks to hours of _____, the party was a success. (prepare)

3. Valerie read the _____ of the French poem. (translate)

4. The _____ of peanut butter and jelly is delicious. (combine)

5. The shape of a bird wing was the _____ behind the new plane design. (inspire)

6. The old pipes gave the water a _____ taste. (metal)

7. Julie demonstrated a great _____ with where all the tools were kept. (familiar)

8. It was so hot outside that we were soon soaked with _____. (perspire)

9. Oiling its wheels increased the cart's _____. (mobile)

10. There's a _____ between my best friend's handwriting and mine. (similar)

Adding the Suffix -ity: Vowel Alternation (/ə/ to Short)

general	individuality	neutral	individual
generality	fatality	original	brutal
neutrality	formal	personality	normal
normality	personal	originality	brutality
formality	fatal	mentality	mental
national	inequal	nationality	inequality

/ə/	Accented
moral	morality

1. Read the paragraph below.
2. Find seven words with the schwa sound and write them on the lines in the first column.
3. Add the suffix -ity to each word and write the new word on the line next to it.
4. Reread all the words and choose one to use in a sentence.

Jess and Tim went to the general meeting for the art contest. They learned that they had to create original pieces and bring them to the library on National Street in two weeks. They decided to make individual pieces rather than work as a team. Both Jess and Tim created artwork that was very personal to them. Jess used neutral colors and painted one of her best paintings ever. Tim used clay to make an outstanding sculpture. At the formal awards ceremony, both Jess and Tim won prizes for their hard work!

/ə/ Words	+ -ity
1.	
2.	
3.	
4.	
5.	
6.	
7.	

Sentence: _____

_____

_____

Adding Suffixes: Vowel Alternation (With Spelling Change)

explanation	explain	proclamation
presumption	deception	reclamation
reception	receive	proclaim
presume	consume	resumption

consumption
reclaim
resume
deceive

Derived -ption					
assumption					

Base -e					
assume					

Derived -ation					
exclamation					

Base -m/-n					
exclaim					

Complete each sentence by adding the suffix -tion to the word in parentheses. (Change the spelling of the base word as necessary.) Write the word on the line.

1. My brother's _____ of vegetables is so large that we have to buy carrots every day. (consume)

2. The magician's first _____ was when she hid the coin in her left hand. (deceive)

3. The king's messenger read a _____ that ended the war. (proclaim)

4. Her _____ helped us understand how to play the game. (explain)

5. The winning team's _____ was heard as soon as the game ended. (exclaim)

6. The _____ of the game began after the rain stopped. (resume)

7. It is a _____ to think you are allowed to enter a home just because a door has been left open. (presume)

8. The _____ of the flooded land began when they pumped out the extra water. (reclaim)

9. Families and school faculty had a _____ to honor students' achievements. (recieve)

10. Making an _____ about someone you don't know very well isn't fair. (assume)

verification	identification	notification
justification	simplify	simplification
verify	identify	magnify
qualify	notify	justify
clarify	clarification	purify
purification	magnification	unify
qualification	unification	multiply
multiplication		

Base -ify/-iply	Derived -ation
classify	classification

1. Read each sentence.

2. Choose one word from the pair in parentheses that best completes the sentence and write it on the line.

3. Place an n above the nouns and a v above the verbs.

---

1. The campers had to _____ the river water before they could drink it. (purify/purification)

2. We received a _____ in the mail that we were prizewinners. (notify/notification)

3. Amy needed further _____ before she understood what to do next. (clarify/clarification)

4. The family decided to _____ their lives by giving away their television. (simplify/simplification)

5. Can you _____ that this is the correct address? (verify/verification)

6. Malcolm had to show his _____ before he could board the airplane. (identify/identification)

7. The _____ was so strong we could see every hair on the beetle's legs. (magnify/magnification)

8. Rosa had a good excuse to _____ her action. (justify/justification)

9. Akina hoped she would _____ for the track finals. (qualify/qualification)

10. The coach hoped to _____ the team's thinking before the first game. (unify/unification)

Suffixes -ic, -ity/-ty, -ous

poisonous	sensitivity	tragic	glamorous
royalty	comic	frailty	vanity
metallic	loyalty	mountainous	historic
realistic	poetic	density	certainty
similarity	glorious	famous	artistic
adventurous	humorous	hazardous	peculiarity

-ic	-ity/-ty	-ous
heroic	creativity	dangerous

1. Sort the words in the box.
2. Write the adjectives in the left column and the nouns in the right column.
3. Look at the words and tell what you discover about them. Which suffixes make adjectives? Which ones make nouns? Write your ideas on the lines below.

comic	humorous	glamorous	famous	realistic	creativity
poetic	certainty	loyalty	artistic	tragic	peculiarity
glorious	royalty	poisonous	vanity	sensitivity	
heroic	hazardous	frailty	similarity	density	

Adjectives	Nouns
1.	1.
2.	2.
3.	3.
4.	4.
5.	5.
6.	6.
7.	7.
8.	8.
9.	9.
10.	10.
11.	11.
12.	12.

What I learned: _____

_____

Sort 18: Suffixes -ic, -ity/-ty, -ous

predictable	agreeable	breakable	visible
punishable	laughable	terrible	remarkable
audible	edible	decipherable	adaptable
possible	profitable	feasible	dependable
compatible	tangible	horrible	legible
invincible	favorable	gullible	preferable

Sort 19: Adding Suffixes -able, -ible

Base + -able	Root + -ible

1. Read the suffix in the center of each web and write the meaning beneath it.
2. Fill in the surrounding ovals with words that end with that suffix.
3. Write the meaning below each word.

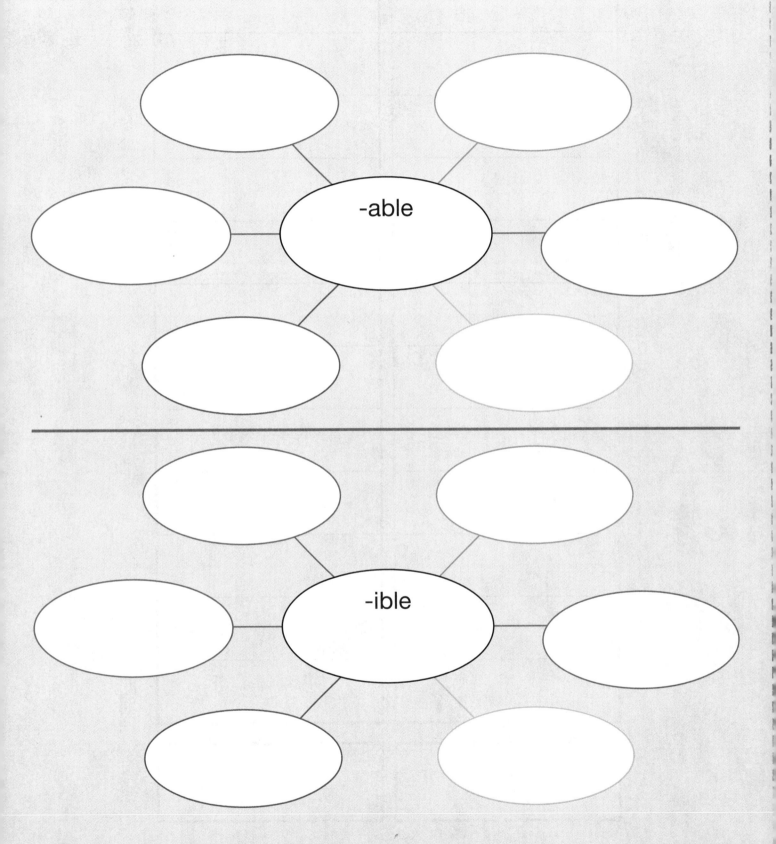

-able

-ible

Sort 19: Adding Suffixes -able, -ible

Adding Suffix -able (With Drop e and No Spelling Change)

comparable	lovable	reusable	desirable
noticeable	pleasurable	consumable	excusable
exchangeable	replaceable	knowledgeable	manageable
believable	rechargeable	changeable	salvageable
traceable	removable	adorable	disposable

Drop e	No Change

Read each base word. Add the suffix -able and write the word on the line. (Drop e as necessary.) Then write a sentence that uses the new word in context.

1. change _____

2. notice _____

3. excuse _____

4. exchange _____

5. consume _____

6. knowledge _____

7. salvage _____

8. manage _____

9. reuse _____

10. love _____

11. compare _____

12. replace _____

Sort 20: Adding Suffix -able (With Drop e and No Spelling Change)

propelled	benefiting	compelling
leveled	occurred	piloting
preferred	limited	modeling
editing	committed	quarreled
repellant	conference	referred
beginning	controlled	excelled
forgetting	exiting	listened

Double	Do Not Double
omitted	orbited

Complete each sentence by adding an ending to the word in parentheses. (Double the final consonant as necessary.) Write the word on the line.

1. The engine _____ the boat forward. (propel)

2. Sue's mother _____ her time on the computer. (limit)

3. Olivia has always _____ peaches to plums. (prefer)

4. The heat was a _____ reason to go inside. (compel)

5. Amy and Cho _____ over who would get to feed the class pet. (quarrel)

6. Ben _____ his temper even after his little brother broke his airplane model. (control)

7. The captain _____ the plane made a perfect landing. (pilot)

8. The teacher _____ several times to her favorite book. (refer)

9. People began _____ the theater once the movie was over. (exit)

10. The bulldozer _____ the hills of dirt on the field. (level)

11. The insect _____ prevented Liam from getting mosquito bites. (repel)

12. The children's hospital is _____ from our school's fundraiser. (benefit)

13. Each student's parents had a _____ with the teacher. (confer)

14. The book group met at the _____, middle, and end of the novel. (begin)

15. With training and practice, Sarah _____ in tennis. (excel)

Sort 21: Accent and Doubling

prejudge	foreword	postpone
afterword	forearm	forecast
afternoon	predate	postscript
postdate	aftertaste	postseason
preschool	predetermine	forewarn
aftershock	aftereffect	prepared
forerunner	foresee	precaution
afterglow	foreshadow	preoccupied

Prefixes pre-, fore-, post-, after-

pre-	fore-	post-	after-
prewar	forethought	postwar	afterthought

1. Write the definition of each prefix.
2. Write a word containing that prefix and its meaning.
3. Draw a picture to illustrate the word you defined.

pre-: _____

Word: _____

Definition: _____

fore-: _____

Word: _____

Definition: _____

post-: _____

Word: _____

Definition: _____

after-: _____

Word: _____

Definition: _____

Sort 22: Prefixes pre-, fore-, post-, after-

Internet	subtotal	overflow	international
overtake	interchange	interact	subhead
overwhelm	overthrow	intersect	interconnect
subway	submerge	subfloor	interfere
subdivide	sublet	subtitle	overlook
overeager	overreact	suburban	intercept
intermediate	overstep	oversee	overripe

inter-	sub-	over-
intermural	subconscious	overrate

1. Choose two prefixes (inter-, sub-, or over-), and write one in the center of each web. Write the meaning below each prefix. (Remember that sub- and over- have more than one meaning.)

2. Fill in the surrounding ovals with words that begin with that prefix.

3. Write the meaning below each word.

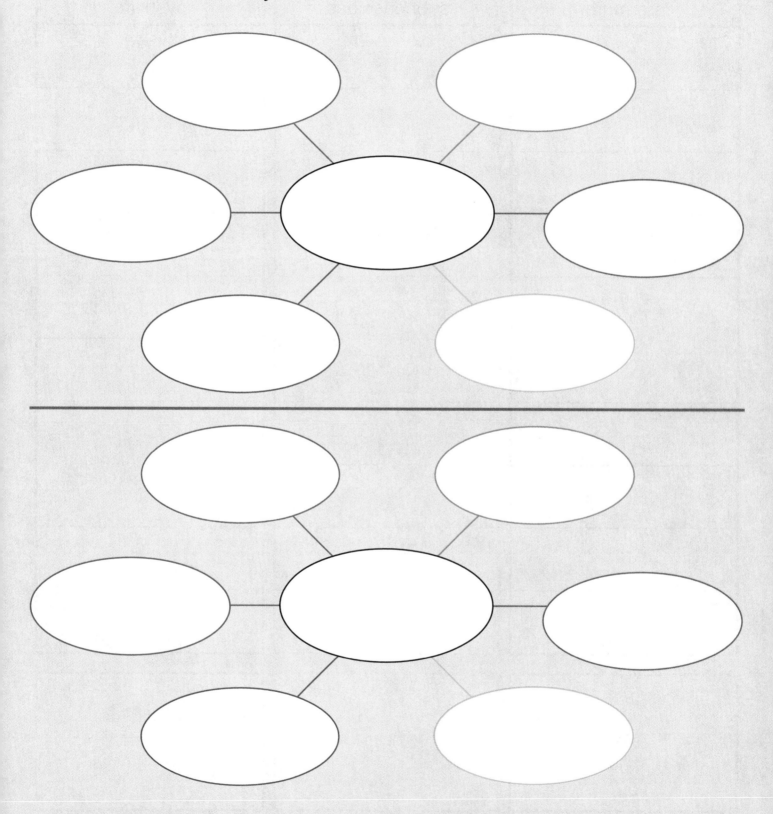

Sort 23: Greek and Latin Prefixes inter-, sub-, over-

Greek and Latin Elements micro-, mega-, super-, hyper-

microfilm	hyperlink	superhero	megahertz	microscope
superhuman	microsurgery	megastar	superhighway	megabyte
superimpose	megahit	microwave	superstar	hypersensitive
megabuck	supernatural	megaton	microchip	hyperextend
megaplex	micrometer	microbiology	supercomputer	hypertext

micro-	mega-	super-	hyper-
microphone	megaphone	supermarket	hyperactive

1. Write the definition of each word element.
2. Write a word containing that element and its meaning.
3. Draw a picture to illustrate the word you defined.

micro-: _____

Word: _____

Definition: _____

mega-: _____

Word: _____

Definition: _____

super-: _____

Word: _____

Definition: _____

hyper-: _____

Word: _____

Definition: _____

Sort 24: Greek and Latin Elements micro-, mega-, super-, hyper-

photograph	symphony	photosynthesis
television	phonograph	telecommunication
telephone	telegraph	telescope
phonics	telephoto	thermometer
barometer	micrometer	centimeter
teleconference	graphic	photocopy
autograph	xylophone	biography
perimeter	telethon	photojournalist

graph	meter

phon	photo	tele

1. Choose two word roots (graph, meter, phon, photo, or tele), and write one in the center of each web. Write the meaning below each prefix.
2. Fill in the surrounding ovals with words that contain that word root.
3. Write the meaning below each word.

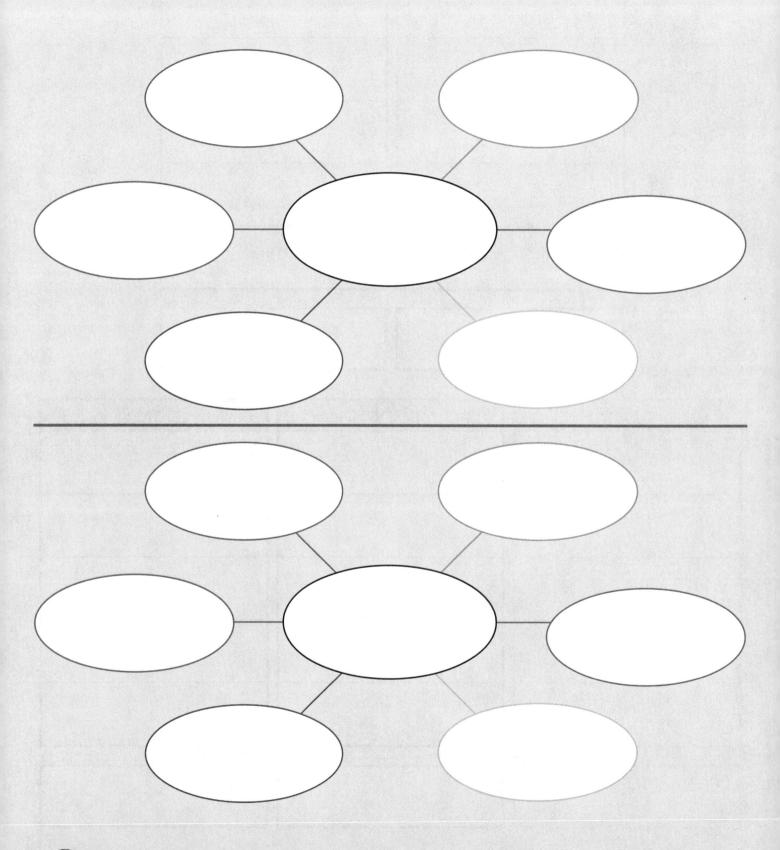

Sort 25: Greek Word Roots graph, meter, phon, photo, tele

inspection	support	portable
perspective	deport	speculate
import	spectator	transport
report	prospect	portfolio
inspector	heliport	spectacle
spectacular	spectrum	opportunity

spect	port
respect	export

1. Read the word root in the center of each web and write the meaning below it.
2. Fill in the surrounding ovals with words that contain that word root.
3. Write the meaning below each word.

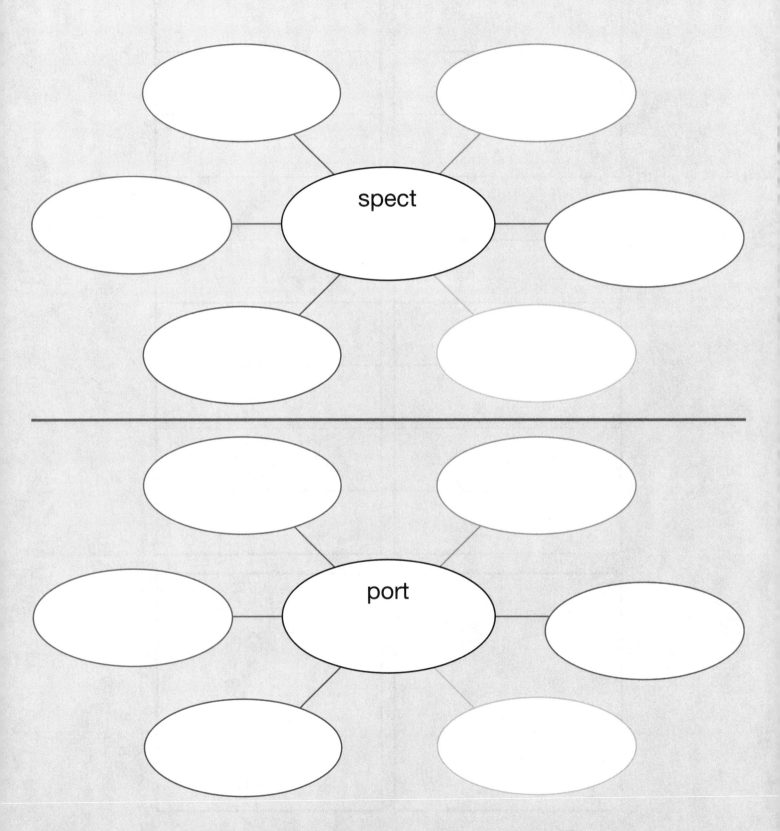

spect

port

 Sort 26: Latin Word Roots spect, port

audible	contradict	auditorium
unpredictable	auditory	verdict
audience	audiotape	dictionary
predict	audition	dictator
audit	diction	audiovisual

Latin Word Roots dic, aud

dic	aud
dictate	audio

1. Write the meaning of each word root next to the headers.
2. Read each word and circle the word root or roots it contains.
3. Write a definition for each word.

dic: _____   **aud:** _____

1. diction _____

2. verdict _____

3. auditory _____

4. predict _____

5. audience _____

6. dictator _____

7. audiotape _____

8. contradict _____

9. auditorium _____

10. unpredictable _____

11. audible _____

12. dictionary _____

13. audition _____

14. audit _____

15. dictate _____

subtract	contract	remote
erupt	distract	promotion
rupture	traction	demote
abrupt	attraction	promote
disrupt	tractor	emotion
motor	corrupt	interruption
bankrupt	extract	motivate

rupt	tract	mot
interrupt	attract	motion

1. Write a definition of each word root.
2. Write a word containing that word root and its meaning.
3. Draw a picture to illustrate the word you defined.

rupt: _____

Word: _____

Definition: _____

tract: _____

Word: _____

Definition: _____

mot: _____

Word: _____

Definition: _____

reject	discredit	injection
eject	objection	manuscript
subject	manage	manufacture
credit	maneuver	credible
projectile	rejection	manicure
manipulate	credentials	

ject	man	cred
inject	manual	incredible

1. Read each sentence.
2. Choose one word from the box that best completes the sentence and write it on the line. (Note: Not all words have to be used and each word can be used only once.)
3. Circle the word root it contains.

reject	eject	manual	maneuver	discredit	manipulate
projectile	objection	manage	credit	rejection	credentials
injection	manuscript	manufacture	credible	subject	inject

1. The factory was built to _____ canned goods.

2. Ally reached up and caught the _____.

3. Rita didn't find Tom's story about killer bugs _____.

4. The doctor hopes a flu _____ will keep the boy healthy.

5. The climber could easily _____ up the mountain.

6. Sam couldn't _____ his store with a broken leg.

7. Maria's _____ to the competition was there wasn't enough time to practice.

8. The pilot had to _____ from the plane when it went out of control.

9. The author spent several years writing the _____ for his novel.

10. My mother asked me to _____ my least favorite paint colors for my room.

11. Together the students worked on the report for their _____.

12. We read the _____ before using the computer.

inscription	revise	scribe
provide	television	visionary
description	vista	transcribe
supervise	video	subscribe
prescribe	prescription	inscribe
visible	visit	transcript
postscript	subscription	televise
improvise		

vid/vis	scrib/script
vision	describe

1. Read each sentence.
2. Choose one word from the pair in parentheses that best completes the sentence and write it on the line.
3. Circle the word root or roots it contains.

1. The _____ on the inside front cover of the book told us to whom it belonged. (subscription/inscription)

2. I will _____ you with equipment for the rock-climbing trip. (provide/visit)

3. Tara picked up her _____ at the pharmacy. (prescription/description)

4. You have to _____ small children very closely. (supervise/televise)

5. I will _____ the writing on the cave wall so we can study it later. (inscribe/transcribe)

6. After Aiden signed the letter, he added a _____ at the bottom. (transcript/postscript)

7. Eduardo painted a picture of a _____ of the lake. (vista/video)

8. The scientist was such a _____ that he spent all day dreaming of new ideas. (visible/visionary)

9. Do you _____ to any magazines about pets? (scribe/subscribe)

10. Katrina's _____ was connected to her stereo and DVD player. (television/vista)

11. The doctor can _____ an antibiotic for the infant's cold. (prescribe/inscribe)

12. Writers and editors worked to _____ the film before the premiere. (revise/televise)

Latin Word Roots jud, leg, flu

legislator	legitimate	judge	flume
flush	prejudge	legislate	illegal
influence	fluent	judicial	judgmental
prejudice	misjudge	legacy	fluctuate
influenza	fluency	privilege	legalize

jud	leg	flu
judgment	legal	fluid

1. Write the meaning of each word root.
2. Read each word and circle the word root it contains.
3. Choose five of the words and write a sentence that uses each word in context.
4. Underline the chosen word in each sentence.

---

jud: _____

leg: _____

flu: _____

1. legislate

2. fluctuate

3. illegal

4. judicial

5. influence

6. prejudge

7. influenza

8. legacy

9. judgmental

10. legitimate

11. fluent

12. legislator

Sentences:

1. _____

_____

2. _____

_____

3. _____

_____

4. _____

_____

5. _____

_____

inspire	resign	conspire
transpire	insist	assist
insistent	perspire	design
assign	aspiration	insignia
signature	consistent	persist
designate	resistance	cosign

spire	sist	sign
expire	resist	signal

1. Read each sentence and the word root in parentheses.
2. Complete each sentence by writing a word that contains that word root.
3. Circle the word root in your word.

1. The builder will follow the architect's _____. (sign)

2. His greatest _____ was to become an astronaut. (spire)

3. The employee had to _____ her old job to take a better one. (sign)

4. Can you _____ that man crossing the street? (sist)

5. We will _____ together to plan a surprise party. (spire)

6. The teacher will _____ you to a group. (sign)

7. I _____ that you join us for dinner. (sist)

8. Nature may _____ you to write a poem. (spire)

9. The long practice session in the hot gymnasium caused Lorraine to _____. (spire)

10. The cake looked so delicious that we could not _____ it. (sist)

11. The bank requires a _____ on the check. (sign)

12. My baby sister has a _____ nap time. (sist)

13. The coach will _____ two team captains. (sign)

14. The rescue crew will _____ in the storm. (sist)

15. Our free movie pass will _____ soon. (spire)

corporate	peddle	peddler
pedal	incorporate	capitol
pedicure	corps	decapitate
captivity	pedestal	centipede
corporal	captive	captivate
corpse	expedition	captain

cap	ped	corp
capital	pedestrian	corporation

1. Write the meaning of each word root.
2. Read each pair of words and circle the word roots in each word.
3. Choose five pairs of words and write a sentence that uses each word pair. For example, The pedestrian packed a backpack and went on a great expedition. (pedestrian/expedition)

cap: _____   ped: _____   corp: _____

Word Pairs

1. pedicure/peddler
2. corporate/corporal
3. captivate/captive
4. pedal/peddle
5. capital/capitol
6. pedestrian/expedition
7. corps/corpse
8. centipede/pedestal

Sentences:

1. _____
_____

2. _____
_____

3. _____
_____

4. _____
_____

5. _____
_____

Sort 33: Greek and Latin Elements cap, ped, corp

divert	insect	landform
format	section	revert
convert	bisect	invert
inform	conversion	formal
conform	advertise	reform
sector	formulate	reverse
universe	uniform	intersect

sect	vert/vers	form
dissect	version	formula

1. Read each sentence.
2. Choose one word from the box that best completes the sentence and write it on the line. (Note: Not all words have to be used and each word can be used only once.)
3. Circle the word root it contains.

divert	section	inform	intersect	formal	sector
conform	advertise	bisect	convert	invert	conversion
formulate	reform	version	revert	insect	uniform

1. The hallways in the school _____ near the lobby.

2. Workers dug a ditch to _____ water from the stream.

3. Maya will _____ her new store in the newspaper.

4. It took the students quite some time to _____ to the school's new dress code.

5. I am learning how to _____ centimeters to meters.

6. Because we know the star of the play, we got to sit in the front _____ of the theater.

7. Do you prefer the old or new _____ of the game?

8. Manuel took the time to _____ a good answer.

9. Tonya wore her finest clothing for the _____ party.

10. Mark's speech will _____ his classmates on the benefits of recycling.

11. The class gathered facts on the largest _____.

12. In math, we learned to _____ shapes.

inactive	immoral	illegal
irremovable	inescapable	immeasurable
illiterate	irrational	incapable
immature	illogical	irresponsible
injustice	immortal	illegitimate
irregular	inaccurate	irresistible
insecure	immigrate	immodest

in-	im-	il-	ir-
incorrect	immobile	illegible	irreplaceable

1. Make new words by adding the prefix in- (in-, im-, il-, or ir-) to the following base words. Write the words on the lines.

measureable	_____	literate	_____
justice	_____	rational	_____
regular	_____	migrate	_____
legal	_____	accurate	_____
mortal	_____	modest	_____
logical	_____	legitimate	_____
active	_____	resistible	_____
escapable	_____	secure	_____
capable	_____	mature	_____
removable	_____	responsible	_____

2. Choose one pair of words, and draw a picture that shows the meaning of the base word and of the base word + prefix.

Base Word: _____

Base Word + Prefix: _____

Sort 35: Prefix Assimilation: Prefixes in-, im-, il-, ir-

Prefix Assimilation: Prefixes com-, col-, con-

combination	concert	collide	combine
collate	compete	connect	collision
congestion	collaborate	competition	congress
conclude	collect	company	committee
companion	commit	colleague	collapse
constellation	conference	congregation	collateral

com-	col-	con-
common	collection	conspire

1. Write the prefix com- in the center of the web.
2. Fill in the surrounding ovals with words that contain that prefix.
3. Think about how each word relates to "coming together" and write the meaning for the word below it.

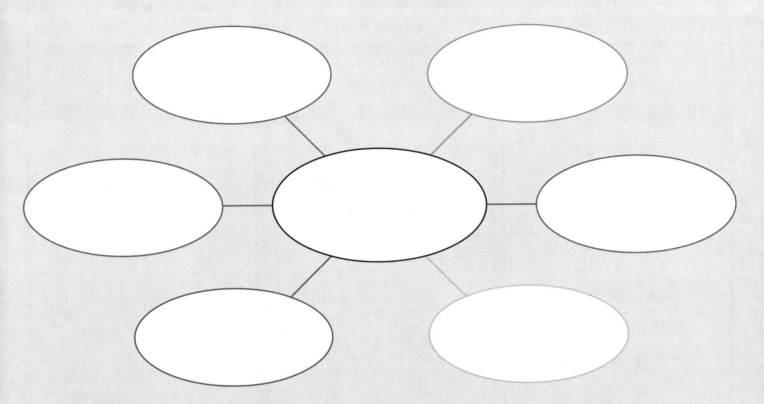

 4. In the box below, list words that begin with com- but that do not mean "coming together," for example, the word comb.

Com- words that do not mean "coming together"

Sort 36: Prefix Assimilation: Prefixes com-, col-, con-

Listen to each word that is read aloud. Match the word to its clue and fill in the spaces of the crossword puzzle.

CLUES

DOWN

1. not fastened to anything
2. stop
3. bad behavior
5. occurring every three months

ACROSS

4. think over again
6. lifted up
7. railway that runs on one rail
8. something that is for both eyes at once
9. to combine into one

Spell Check 1a: Inflected Ending -ed and Prefixes

1. Listen to each word as it is read aloud. Write the words on the lines.

2. Draw a line from the word to its antonym—a word that means the opposite. (Note: Use each antonym only once.)

Words	Antonyms
1. _____	fullest
2. _____	messiness
3. _____	dirtiest
4. _____	worthlessness
5. _____	milder
6. _____	meanest
7. _____	rudeness
8. _____	dullest
9. _____	carefulness
10. _____	more ordinary
11. _____	with little to do
12. _____	lightness
13. _____	easiest
14. _____	clumsy
15. _____	talkative
16. _____	louder
17. _____	ugly
18. _____	later

 Spell Check 1b: Suffixes

1. Listen to each word as it is read aloud. Write the word on the line.
2. Write a definition for the word.
3. Write a sentence using the word.
4. In the space provided, draw a picture that connects to the word.

SPELL CHECK 2a

Spell: _____

Define: _____

_____

_____

Sentence: _____

_____

_____

_____

Draw:

Spell: _____

Define: _____

_____

_____

Sentence: _____

_____

_____

_____

Draw:

Listen to each word as it is read aloud. Write the words on the lines.

1. _____

2. _____

3. _____

4. _____

5. _____

6. _____

7. _____

8. _____

9. _____

10. _____

11. _____

12. _____

13. _____

14. _____

15. _____

16. _____

17. _____

18. _____

19. _____

20. _____

Choose three different words and use each one in a separate sentence. Then circle the target words.

1. _____

2. _____

3. _____

1. Listen to each word as it is read aloud. Write the words on the lines.

2. Draw a line from the word to its synonym—a word or words that mean the same or nearly the same. (Note: Use each synonym only once.)

Words	Synonyms
1.	family
2.	exact
3.	catch fire
4.	pillar
5.	correction
6.	tell
7.	pick
8.	dampen
9.	speed
10.	quit
11.	contest
12.	thankfulness
13.	lawbreaker
14.	fall apart
15.	explain
16.	dweller
17.	ceremony
18.	inhale

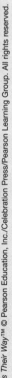

1. Listen to each word as it is read aloud. Write the words on the lines.
2. For words 1–9, draw a line from the word to its synonym—a word that means the same or nearly the same. (Note: Use each synonym only once.)
3. For words 10–18, draw a line from the word to its antonym—a word or words that mean the opposite. (Note: Use each antonym only once.)

Words	Synonyms
1. _____	plan
2. _____	disagreement
3. _____	evenhanded
4. _____	against
5. _____	mixture
6. _____	regularity
7. _____	excite
8. _____	tinny
9. _____	sweat

Words	Antonyms
10. _____	casual
11. _____	gentleness
12. _____	specific
13. _____	strange
14. _____	unmovable
15. _____	favoritism
16. _____	drive apart
17. _____	difference
18. _____	copy

Listen to each word as it is read aloud. Write the words on the lines.

1. _____
2. _____
3. _____
4. _____
5. _____
6. _____
7. _____
8. _____
9. _____
10. _____

11. _____
12. _____
13. _____
14. _____
15. _____
16. _____
17. _____
18. _____
19. _____
20. _____

Choose three different words and use each one in a separate sentence. Then circle the target words.

1. _____
2. _____
3. _____

Listen to each word that is read aloud. Match the word to its clue and fill in the spaces of the crossword puzzle.

SPELL CHECK 5

CLUES

DOWN
2. able to be eaten
3. able to be saved
7. weakness
9. that can be read easily

ACROSS
1. condition of being aware of others' feelings
4. wanting or craving
5. fascinating
6. very sad
8. pleasant

1. Listen to each group of words as it is read aloud.
2. Pick a word from each group and write one in each box.
3. Write the meaning of each word.
4. Write a sentence using the word.

Spell: _____

Define: _____

Sentence: _____

Spell: _____

Define: _____

Sentence: _____

Spell: _____

Define: _____

Sentence: _____

Spell: _____

Define: _____

Sentence: _____

Spell Check 6: Greek and Latin Elements

1. Listen to each word as it is read aloud. Write the words on the lines.
2. Circle any roots you see in the words.

1. _____   11. _____

2. _____   12. _____

3. _____   13. _____

4. _____   14. _____

5. _____   15. _____

6. _____   16. _____

7. _____   17. _____

8. _____   18. _____

9. _____   19. _____

10. _____   20. _____

Write three different roots and their definitions on the lines below.

1. Root: _____   Definition: _____

2. Root: _____   Definition: _____

3. Root: _____   Definition: _____

1. Listen to each word as it is read aloud. Write the word on the line.
2. Write a definition for the word.
3. Write a sentence using the word.
4. In the space provided, draw a picture that connects to the word.

Spell: _____

Define: _____

_____

_____

Sentence: _____

_____

_____

Draw:

Spell: _____

Define: _____

_____

_____

Sentence: _____

_____

_____

Draw:

Listen to each word as it is read aloud. Write the word in the box that shows the word element it contains. Then circle the element in each word.

SPELL
CHECK
8a

vid/vis	scrib/script

jud	leg	flu

SPELL CHECK 8b

1. Listen to each word as it is read aloud.
2. Write the words on the lines.
3. Circle any Greek or Latin elements you see in the words.

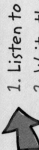

1. _____
2. _____
3. _____
4. _____
5. _____
6. _____
7. _____
8. _____
9. _____

10. _____
11. _____
12. _____
13. _____
14. _____
15. _____
16. _____
17. _____
18. _____

Choose three words that each contain a different element and write definitions for them on the lines below.

1. Word: _____   Definition: _____
2. Word: _____   Definition: _____
3. Word: _____   Definition: _____

Listen to each word as it is read aloud. Write each word in the box under the prefix it contains. Circle the prefix in each word.

in

ir

com